ANGELFISH

A TRUE BOOK

by
Elaine Landau

Children's Press®
A Division of Grolier Publishing

New York London Hong Kong Sydney
Danbury, Connecticut

Reading Consultant
Linda Cornwell
Learning Resource Consultant
Indiana Department
of Education

A freshwater
angelfish

Visit Children's Press® on the
Internet at:
http://publishing.grolier.com

Library of Congress Cataloging-in-Publication Data

Landau, Elaine.
    Angelfish / by Elaine Landau.
        p.   cm. — (A True book)
    Includes bibliographical references and index.
    Summary: Distinguishes saltwater from freshwater angelfish, describes the
latter, and suggests how to care for this popular pet in a home aquarium.
    ISBN: 0-516-20660-5 (lib. bdg.) 0-516-26488-5 (pbk.)
    1. Freshwater angelfishes—Juvenile literature. [1. Angelfish. 2.
Aquarium fishes.] I. Title. II. Series.
SF458.A5L35   1999
639.3`772—dc21   98-16121
                                                                        CIP
                                                                        AC

GROLIER
PUBLISHING

Contents

The Blue Moon saltwater angelfish is found in the waters of the Red Sea.

Angelfish

What popular aquarium fish is known for its attractive coloring and its unusual shape? It's a heavenly creature called an angelfish. Many different fish are called angelfish. Some are marine, or saltwater, angelfish. They live in the warm tropical seas around coral reefs. They

A yellow saltwater angelfish (above) swims along a coral reef in the south Pacific. The Emperor angelfish (right) is one of the largest species of salt-water angelfish.

are believed to be among the world's most colorful fish.

Saltwater angelfish often can be found in public aquariums

or exotic pet shops. They are not usually found in home aquariums because they grow quite large.

Other types of angelfish live only in freshwater. These angelfish are found in the waters surrounding South America's Amazon River Basin. Freshwater angelfish were first taken to Germany from South America in 1911. Ten years later, in 1921, they were brought to the United States.

Freshwater angelfish in
the Amazon River Basin

Since that time they have
become a favorite among people here.

This book is about freshwater angelfish. You may have
already seen these appealing,

or interesting, fish in a friend's fish tank or in a pet store. And if you have an aquarium at home, you may even have an angelfish of your own!

A freshwater angelfish looking at its reflection in an aquarium.

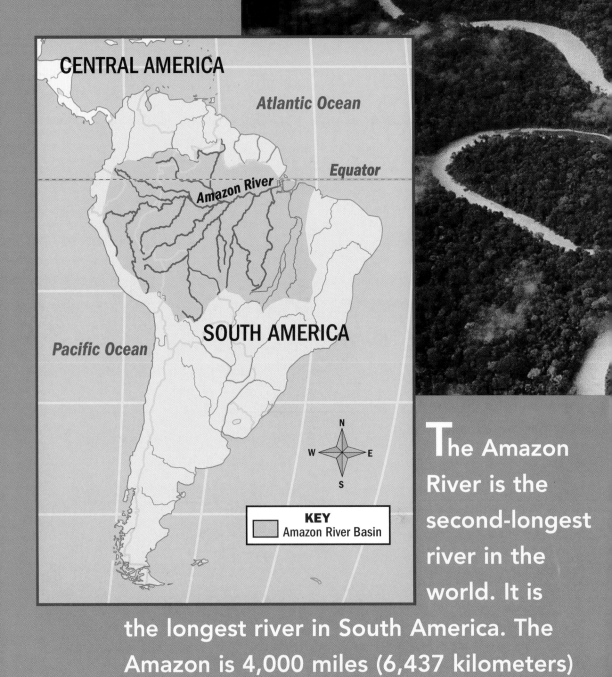

CENTRAL AMERICA

Atlantic Ocean

Equator

Amazon River

SOUTH AMERICA

Pacific Ocean

N
W   E
S

KEY
Amazon River Basin

The Amazon River is the second-longest river in the world. It is the longest river in South America. The Amazon is 4,000 miles (6,437 kilometers)

The Amazon River Basin

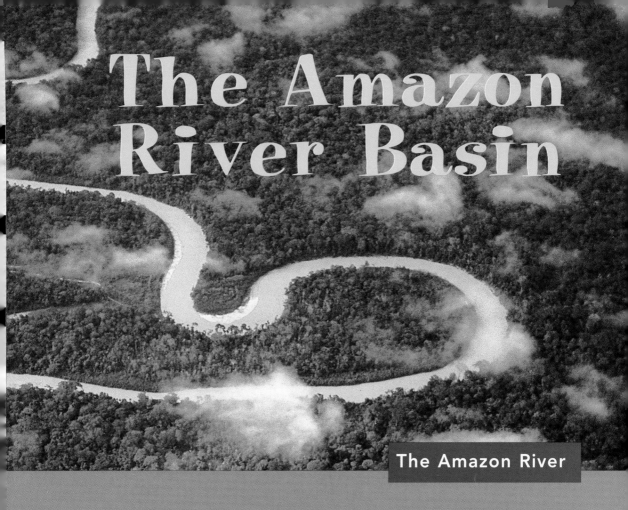

The Amazon River

long. The Amazon River Basin is the area of land that surrounds the river and its tributaries. (A tributary is a smaller river that flows into a larger river.) Water drains from this area into the Amazon. The Amazon River Basin covers about 2,700,000 square miles (7,000,000 square kilometers).

A Popular Fish

Freshwater angelfish are fun to watch. They are curious fish that like to see what's going on in their underwater world. Many people enjoy watching them swim in fish tanks. Freshwater angelfish swim in a slow, majestic way. They almost seem to march slowly through the water.

These children are enjoying the movements of the fish in a tank.

Freshwater angelfish are about 5 to 6 inches (13 to 15 centimeters) long. They have a thin, oval-shaped body and long, pointed fins. Their fins jut out so far that the fish

The long fins of the freshwater angelfish give it its triangle shape.

look almost triangular. In the wild, freshwater angelfish are silver colored with thick black bars running up and down their bodies. The iris, or colored part, of this fish's eyes is red.

The body of an angelfish looks somewhat flattened. Some people jokingly say that an angelfish looks as though someone sat on it. But the fish's narrow shape is useful in its watery environment. It

The bright red iris is visible on this leopard angelfish (above). The black bars, or stripes, on a freshwater angelfish make it easy to spot (right).

helps the fish to swim faster, and also lets it fit into small spaces. This can be helpful when hunting for food or escaping from an enemy.

People who breed freshwater angelfish have produced some beautiful and popular new varieties, or types. Among these varieties are the golden angelfish, which is prized for its lovely gold color. The half-black angelfish is another popular choice. Part of its body is

The half-black angelfish (left) and the golden angelfish (right) are popular in home aquariums.

silver colored, and part is black. And the angelfish known as the black lace angel has dark markings that make it look like it's wearing black

Favorite varieties of freshwater angelfish include the black lace angelfish (left) and the pure black angelfish (right).

lace. The pure black angel is still another type of freshwater angelfish. The entire fish, including its fins and tail, is black.

The blushing angelfish is another freshwater variety.

These and other new kinds of freshwater angelfish are much in demand. However, these fish tend to be weaker than other angelfish. They also cost more money to buy.

Keeping Freshwater Angelfish

For many reasons, people who keep fish like their freshwater angelfish best. These fish do well in tanks with several different kinds of fish. But adult freshwater angelfish should never be kept in the same tank as small fish such as

It is safe for angelfish to share the same aquarium with most other fish.

guppies and tetras because the angelfish are likely to eat them. It is okay to place younger—and smaller— angelfish together in a tank with most other fish. But avoid putting small fish in the tank that an angelfish could swallow whole.

When choosing tankmates for your angelfish, it is best to select other peaceful fish. Fierce or unfriendly fish might

The long fins of the freshwater angelfish are easy targets for unfriendly fish.

Ask a worker in a pet store if you are unsure about tankmates for your angelfish.

nip the angelfish's long fins. People who work in pet shops can usually give you good advice on which fish get along well together.

Many other fish destroy aquarium plants or dig up the tank's gravel, but freshwater

Angelfish are easy to keep because they don't damage or destroy their surroundings.

angelfish do not damage aquarium setups. These fish also become quite tame and get used to having humans look at them. Some people even claim that their freshwater angelfish eagerly await their feeding time!

Nevertheless, if you are thinking of getting a freshwater angelfish, you should keep some basic things in mind. The fish you buy may be very young. It will need room to grow. Freshwater angelfish should be kept in aquariums that provide plenty of room for swimming. The sides of the tank should be high because these long-finned fish are sometimes taller than they are long. The tank

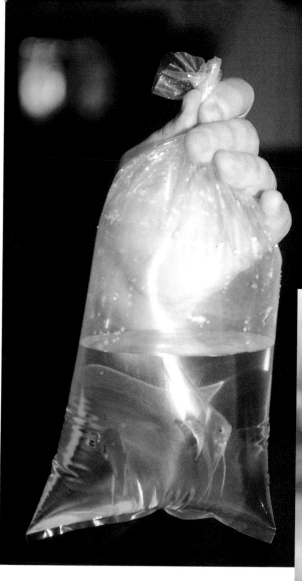

These angelfish (left) are ready to be moved from a pet store to a customer's home aquarium. The fins of this young angelfish (right) will get much longer before it is fully grown.

should have some tall broad-leaf plants, too. (A broadleaf plant is a plant that has wide leaves.)

Freshwater angelfish come from tropical areas. This means that they come from the extremely hot area of Earth near the equator. Since the water in tropical seas is warm, the ideal temperature in an angelfish's tank would

A freshwater angelfish in its aquarium tank

be 70 to 85 degrees Fahrenheit (21 to 29 degrees Celsius). But these fish can survive in temperatures ranging from 65 to 90 degrees Fahrenheit (18 to 32 degrees Celsius). However, any temperature change must be made gradually (slowly). It is also important to remember that fish need more food, space, and oxygen in higher water temperatures.

Freshwater angelfish will eat many of the prepared and frozen fish foods sold in pet

shops. But they should be fed live foods regularly. Brine shrimp, a type of shrimp that is often used for this purpose, are sold in many pet shops.

Starting Your

Here is the basic equipment you need to start your own aquarium:

Fish tank and cover
Filter
Air pump
Heater
Thermometer

- A tank that holds 10 to 20 gallons (38 to 76 liters) of water is a good place to start. The tank cover should include a lamp that will shine down into the tank.

A brand-new fish tank and cover

- Filters remove dirt from the water and keep it clean.

An aquarium filter at work

Own Aquarium

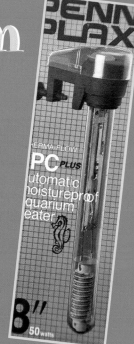

One brand of heater

- An electric air pump pushes water through the filter.

- A heater keeps the water warm. It must be the right temperature for the fish to stay healthy.

- The thermometer indicates the water temperature.

This thermometer shows the water temperature is about 78 degrees F (25 degrees C).

Ask an adult to help you set up your aquarium. You can find more information in the To Find Out More section of this book, as well as at your local pet store.

Breeding

Freshwater angelfish are good breeders. This means that they mate often and produce many young. People who breed these fish claim that one pair of angelfish can produce five thousand to ten thousand young in one year!

In this fish hatchery (a place where eggs are hatched), thousands of fish are produced each year.

The tall plants that surround this angelfish may be the perfect breeding ground.

Angelfish seem to prefer a tall broadleaf plant as a breeding ground. But in some cases the fish may set their eggs on a rock or a piece of wood. Angelfish have even been known to put their eggs on the glass sides of their aquarium tanks.

The female angelfish usually lays out a large number of eggs for the male to fertilize. Sometimes there may be as many as one thousand eggs. Both the male and female angelfish take care of the fertilized eggs. They fan fresh water over them and remove

Angelfish use their fins and tails to fan water over their eggs.

any eggs that become cov-
ered with fungi. (Fungi are
plants that have no leaves,
flowers, or roots.)

The adult angelfish chews off the egg's outer casing so that the fry, or baby fish, can get out. Once the egg's shell is broken, the adult angelfish spits out the young fish onto a new leaf. The fry remains on the leaf for a while. Eventually, a gland on the head of the baby fish gives off a threadlike substance. This substance attaches the fry to the leaf. Soon, the adults take the young fish deeper in the water. By the fourth or fifth day, a young angelfish is ready to swim. Their parents then lead it on a swim through the water before the angelfish goes off on its own.

It may seem that angelfish enjoy an ideal family life. But remember that these are fish, not humans. One or both angelfish parents may eat some of the young they have produced. To keep this from

A young black lace angelfish swims on its own.

happening, breeders often separate the parents and the fry.

A large number of fresh-water angelfish are bred and sold in the United States every year. People who keep fish are always anxious to add new specimens, or types, to their collections. Under the right conditions, these graceful and beautiful fish can bring hours of pleasure to all who see them.

Angelfish
are interesting
creatures.

To Find Out More

Here are some additional resources to help you learn more about angelfish and aquariums:

 **Books**

Ancona, George. **The Aquarium Book.** Clarion Books, 1994.

Aronsky, Jim. **Crinkleroot's 25 Fish Every Child Should Know.** Bradbury Press, 1993.

Bailey, Donna. **Fish.** Raintree Steck-Vaughn, 1990.

Brenner, Barbara and Bernice Chardiet. **Where's That Fish?** Scholastic, 1994.

Cole, Joanna. **The Magic School Bus on the Ocean Floor.** Scholastic, 1992.

Landau, Elaine. **Your Pet Tropical Fish.** Children's Press, 1997.

Organizations and Online Sites

Angelfish
http://www.colorpro.com/ angels

Full-color photographs of different kinds of angelfish and answers to FAQs.

FINS
http://www.actwin.com/fish

FINS is the Fish Information Service—an archive of information about aquariums, including sites specific to angelfish.

FishAmerica Foundation
1033 North Fairfax
Suite 20
Alexandria, VA 22314

Fish and Wildlife Reference Service
5430 Grosvenor Lane
Suite 110
Bethesda, MD 20814

Index of Aquariums
http://www.aquae.com

Information about public aquariums throughout the world, with links to educational resources, databases, photographs, and more.

Important Words

aquarium glass tank used to hold plants, fish, or small animals

breed to produce a particular type of animal

coral reef a strip made of coral and other materials that have solidified into rock, usually found close to the ocean's surface

environment surroundings

fertilize to begin reproduction

freshwater water that does not contain salt

nip small bite

Index

Meet the Author

Elaine Landau has a Bachelor of Arts degree in English and Journalism from New York University and a Masters degree in Library and Information Science from Pratt Institute. She has worked as a newspaper reporter, children's book editor, and a youth services librarian, but especially enjoys writing for young people.

Ms. Landau has written more than one hundred nonfiction books on various topics. She lives in Miami, Florida, with her husband Norman and son, Michael.